636.1
S58lw

DETROIT PUBLIC LIBRARY

W9-COL-283

WHAT YOUR
HORSE NEEDS

— By Betsy Sikora Siino —

A Dorling Kindersley Book

MAR 2001

Forelock — Mane — Withers — Hip

Nostril — Dock

Muzzle

Breast — Tail

Flank — Point of hock

Stifle

Fetlock joint — Ergot

Pastern — Heel

Hoof — Coronet

WHAT YOUR HORSE NEEDS

	Less	1	2	3	4	5	More
Time commitment					✓		
Exercise					✓		
Play time			✓				
Space requirements					✓		
Grooming (depending on breed)				✓			
Feeding				✓			
Cleaning up					✓		
Life span				✓			
Good with kids 5 to 10		✓					
Good with kids 10 and over			✓				

MAY - - 2001

CONTENTS

FOREWORD BY BRUCE FOGLE, DVM

Thinking of getting a horse? It's a marvelous idea, although for most of us it's also a major league fantasy rather than a practical possibility. After all, a typical horse is about eight times bigger than you or me. Unlike other companion animals, housing, feeding, and exercising a horse all are logistical and financial burdens few can overcome. Still, we can dream.

Until this century the horse was both our major form of transportation and the engine of agriculture, helping to plow fields or pull loads. Today, throughout North America and Europe, the horse is overwhelmingly a family companion, used for pleasure rather than work.

More than with any other animal companion, a good relationship is based upon your understanding how your horse thinks. You cannot and should not use force to get a horse to do something. Nor should you let her coerce you, by threatening to bite for example, into doing what she wants you to do. Your relationship with your horse must develop, ever so gradually, as one of mutual respect.

This is best achieved with the help of knowledgeable people who understand that there is never a need to "break" a horse. Rather, work with a horse's natural behavior. Learn to understand her body language, to know what she is thinking. This form of training is called positive reinforcement and is what good trainers use to train other species of animals, from parrots, to cats, to dogs, to killer whales.

Horses are highly social animals. We should respect their emotional as well as physical and environmental needs, and train and equip them to live in what is often a restricted environment where there are many unexpected stresses and challenges. Getting off to the right start is the best preventive medicine I can suggest. This little book helps set you on a proper course towards what I hope will be a fruitful rewarding relationship with your horse.

AN ANCIENT PARTNERSHIP

It's a safe bet that were it not for the horse, we humans as a species would not be where we are today. Since about six thousand years ago, when we decided it might be wise to harness the immense talents of the equine species for our own purposes, we have relied on horses to be our transportation, our workmates, our partners in war, and – although we may not always have been willing to admit it – our companions. Looking back, we can't help but wonder what we would have done without them.

Various peoples of Europe and Asia are credited with originally domesticating the horse. They first thought of the animals as a source of food and hides, and then decided horses might be useful for more utilitarian, long-term uses as well. They took horses in from the wild and began breeding them for specific purposes. The results of their efforts, which would ultimately take hold across the globe, are the hundreds of breeds that today inhabit our world – horses bred for all manner of human endeavor, from farming to logging to hauling to hunting to driving to racing to competition jumping, and anything else our very active imaginations can conjure up.

ENDLESS VARIETY

That imagination, and the horse's natural evolution, has blossomed into the countless breeds that occupy the planet today. We have what we call hot-blooded breeds, cold-blooded, warm-blooded, and everything in between, including the beloved "grade" horse, the product of a mixed pedigree. These terms to do not actually refer to the horse's blood, but to her character. Hot-blooded horses – the Thoroughbred and the Arabian being the legends of this group – are best reserved for experienced horse people. The cold-bloods are the big, even-tempered, working-class draft breeds, The warmbloods are a combination of hot and cold, resulting in the talented, even-tempered athletes who today dominate the Olympic riding disciplines.

The immense success we have enjoyed from our domestication of, and subsequent partnership with, this mighty species has stemmed from the character of the horse itself. As members of a very social species, wild, feral, and even domestic horses allowed to live at liberty have occupied the deserts of Africa, the Middle East, and the United States; the rugged cliffs of the British Isles; the more primitive environs of France; and the outback of Australia. Horses have proven themselves to be rugged survivalists, able to withstand some of the harshest environments, thanks to both their sturdy constitutions and their very communal social structures that revolve around a philosophy of teamwork and camaraderie.

Each breed boasts a unique story, from the ponies of the British Isles who were sculpted naturally in rugged, sparse terrain and used their keen intelligence to outwit predators and eradication efforts by humans, to the aristocratic hot-blooded Thoroughbred racehorses of Britain, to the high-powered Olympic warmblood athletes of Europe who were nurtured to perfection like fine works of art, to the versatile cow ponies of the United States who made western expansion possible. These horses' stories are the stuff of which adventure novels are made. And we are privileged to be a part of the adventure.

The diminutive Shetland Pony and the working Shire Horse illustrate the glorious variety found among horses.

SOCIAL BUT WARY

The equine species has been quite successful in the art of survival, primarily because, whether in a wild or domestic environment, the horse has always understood just who and what she is: a prey animal. Though strong, stunning and majestic, she knows she is a favorite target of virtually any large predator. Understand this fact yourself and you take an important step toward successful care of and communication with your horse.

Suddenly it all makes sense. You understand why your horse shies at the sight of a strangely shaped rock on the trail, or why she is wary of every rustle of a leaf. In the wild, an alert mind, coupled with keen senses and the impulse to flee at the first hint of danger (an impulse instantly contagious to all others in the herd), are what keep a horse alive. And because old habits die hard, domestic horses carry on the traditions that for millennia spelled survival for their species. Those who respect such equine traditions are better prepared to become effective caretakers of, and companions to, the horse. And what a rewarding experience that can be!

Horses live in social groups, but they're very picky about who they accept into the group.

You should also be aware that your challenging charge is a very social character, most comfortable with an extended network of buddies about: you, other horses (but only those she deems worthy of being a part of her inner circle), and perhaps a friendly barn cat or dog. Even a goat has been known to become a trusted companion of a horse. You may also notice a territorial streak in your horse from time to time, perhaps when she offers an unfriendly greeting to the new horse in the paddock next door or doesn't appreciate sharing the bathing area with another horse at the stable.

Horses living naturally, whether wild or domestic, tend to live in herds, traditionally comprised of one stallion and a band of mares and their young (a harem set-up, if you will). The horses in a herd spend their days and nights together in family groups, grazing, dozing, frolicking, and looking out for each other – each prepared to alert the others should she suspect that danger may be about.

The communal living situations we humans typically choose for our own social structure are therefore familiar to horses, especially when we have taken the time to commune with them and care for them in a way that honors their own native instincts and habits.

THINGS TO THINK ABOUT

Bringing a new horse into your life is quite different from the experience of bringing other types of animals in. Although a horse can be a great companion, she offers a whole unique set of challenges to her caretaker. This becomes evident as you begin to consider how you will be housing your horse. It's the first important decision you must make once you decide to bring a horse into your life. After all, she can't stay in your room!

HORSE HOUSING

Housing must, of course, be arranged before you bring the horse home, and the nature of it depends on your own housing situation. If you live on spacious acreage zoned for horse ownership, your horse can live on-site with you. But if you're like most horse owners, you will need to make arrangements for her to stay elsewhere.

This may be on a private individual's "horse property," where the horse stays but you take all responsibility for caring for her, or, more commonly, at a boarding stable where resident horses are groomed and ridden by their owners, and their daily needs (feeding, stall cleaning, and so on) are tended to in part by the stable staff.

HOW WILL YOU GET HER?

Once you have decided where your horse will live, you must figure out how to get her there. If you do not own a horse trailer yourself, the person from whom you are purchasing the animal may be able to deliver her. More often, you will have to arrange transportation for her yourself. Ask other horse people for recommendations, especially if you will be boarding your horse in a communal stable. Your colleagues in horse ownership can recommend either a horse transportation company, or perhaps a fellow horse owner who has a trailer and is willing to help you out. Either way, be aware that this will probably mark only the first of the many expenses you will be incurring as a horse owner.

A VETERINARIAN AND A FARRIER

The horse-owner network will also come in handy in your search for a veterinarian and a farrier, or blacksmith, for your horse. You'll no doubt see these professionals plying their crafts at a busy boarding stable, because these are two callings that require their practitioners to make house calls. Their presence also offers you the opportunity to see for yourself how they handle the horses in their care. Most of your fellow horse owners will be able to supply you with recommendations (and warnings), as well.

Make your search for a veterinarian and farrier an important addition to your horse-ownership preparation list. You will want to make sure you have the necessary professionals lined up long before you ever need their services – and preferably before your horse is delivered to her new home.

WHAT YOU NEED TO BUY

You'll have plenty of equipment and supplies to collect before your equine companion comes home. Specifically what you need will depend on where your horse will be living and what you intend to do with her.

Whether you plan to enlist your horse as a friendly partner on the trail, take lessons in a particular discipline, or take your charge into the competitive show ring, it's probably not important that you have all that equipment ready as soon as your horse arrives. In fact, it may actually be better to wait a bit to collect your riding tack until after you get to know your horse better and, perhaps with input from your riding instructor, buy a saddle that fits properly, the right bit, and any other equipment that will be appropriate for you and your riding goals.

But there are some items that you must have ready for your horse's arrival. These include a combination of everyday care necessities (feed and grooming supplies) and basic tack (halter and lead rope). Of course, if your horse will be staying at a boarding stable, you probably won't have to supply her hay, bedding materials and such, but it won't hurt to have treats and any special grains or other elements of her diet handy.

Cleaning out the stall will require of variety of shovels, rakes, and pitchforks. If you board your horse, the stable may have these tools on hand.

A SHOPPING LIST

Assuming that your horse will be living at a traditional boarding facility, the following list should give you an idea of the basic tack and supplies you may want to collect before your horse arrives. If your horse will be living at home with you, add such items as a large shipment of fresh hay, a wheelbarrow, and bedding materials to the list:

○ Properly fitting halter and lead rope
○ Grooming equipment (brushes, curry comb, mane-and-tail brush, hoof pick)
○ Towels, cloths, and sponges
○ Equine first-aid kit
○ Blanket (if your horse will be blanketed at night)
○ Fly halter and fly spray
○ Rake, shovel, pitchfork, manure fork (to rearrange your horse's bedding and hay and to clean up manure, even if these chores are to be handled by barn staff)
○ Two or three plastic buckets
○ Boots or similarly protective footwear (steel-toed riding shoes, for instance) for yourself to protect your feet from equine hooves.
○ Treats (carrots or apples to sweeten your new horse's welcome)

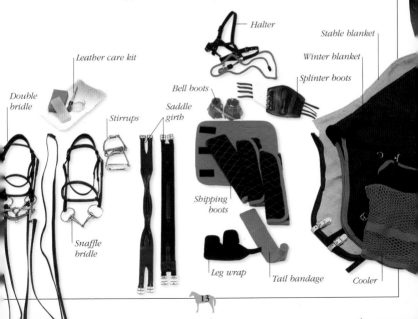

Halter

Stable blanket

Leather care kit

Winter blanket

Splinter boots

Double bridle

Bell boots

Saddle girth

Stirrups

Shipping boots

Snaffle bridle

Leg wrap

Tail bandage

Cooler

BOARDING YOUR HORSE

Living with a horse is an incredibly rewarding experience, but it is also a major responsibility. You have many choices to make, the first of which is where your horse will live.

If, like many horse owners today, you cannot keep your horse on your own property, you will need to depend on a private individual who rents out space to fellow horse owners, or on a commercially run boarding stable. In either of these situations, you will need to think about how your horse will live: at pasture, in a box stall, in an open stall-type shelter with a small pen or paddock area in which to stretch her legs, or a combination of these.

While you will probably be the sole caretaker of a horse who lives with you, your responsibilities in the daily care of your horse can vary in an off-site living situation, depending on the arrangements you make. You may agree to take on the full responsibility of caring for your horse (daily feeding, stall mucking, and such), or your monthly fee may cover partial or full care by the stable staff.

Cost should be only one factor when you decide on a particular boarding situation for your horse. Your peace of mind and your horse's long-term well-being depend on you choosing a safe, clean, well-run facility for your equine companion. Ask other horse owners for recommendations, visit the places yourself, be critically honest in your evaluations, and don't be afraid to change your mind if you decide that a particular barn is not the right home for your horse after all. Your horse is depending on you to make the right decision.

WHAT TO LOOK FOR IN A BOARDING STABLE

Whether you go with a private individual or a commercial operation, certain elements are critical to ensure that your horse lands in the proper living situation. Look for the following when choosing a home for your horse:

○ All-around clean premises occupied by contented, healthy-looking horses.
○ Manure and soiled bedding are removed regularly (either by boarders or staff) and transported an ample distance from the equine living areas.

○ Flies and odor are kept to a minimum through routine hygiene efforts.
○ Water troughs and automatic waterers are kept clean and filled (and monitored during the winter. when they're prone to freezing).
○ Rules of conduct for boarders, visitors, and staff are posted and enforced.
○ A strict no smoking policy is enforced both outdoors and in the barn areas.
○ Clean, fresh feed is offered to horses on time, as requested by each owner.
○ Fire alarms and extinguishers are present both outdoors and in the barn areas.
○ Fresh bedding is supplied regularly.
○ Hay nets, hay racks, or feeders are in the stalls for mealtimes.
○ There is secure fencing, gates, structures and hardware, all properly and regularly maintained.
○ Turn-out and riding rings, pastures, and grooming areas are properly maintained.
○ Individual tack sheds are available for boarders.
○ Low turnover of boarders and positive word-of-mouth.

YOUR HORSE AT HOME

If you're one of the fortunate few who has the space (and the zoning) to keep your horse at home, you will have even greater peace of mind, because you have the luxury of actually living with your horse as a true companion. Such an arrangement offers you the opportunity to keep an eye on your horse and know that all is well, that your horse is content and healthy. Should a problem arise, you are there to call the veterinarian sooner than might be done (especially overnight) in an off-site boarding facility.

But living with a horse requires you to exercise a mighty work ethic each and every day. The responsible care of so large an animal and the proper maintenance of her home requires a great deal of work and time. You will be responsible not only for the daily grooming, exercise and feeding of your horse – which you might be at a boarding stable, too – but also for keeping the proper supplies of hay, feed, and bedding materials in stock. It will also be your job to keep your horse's bedding – the classic equine bed consisting of a clean supply of straw or shavings kept in a comfortably thick layer over an easy-to-clean rubber mat – properly maintained.

In a boarding stable, depending on your arrangement, you might be able to rely on the barn staff to help you out with routine changing and cleaning of the bedding, the daily removal of manure, and the daily watering and multiple feedings a horse requires, as well as ensuring there is always an ample supply of hay and grain on hand. But when you are your horse's full-time caretaker, the responsibility, all of it, is yours: the feeding and watering, the stall mucking, the constant vigilance to ensure that the horse and the grounds are safe. You'll learn quickly why horse people tend to be early risers, especially when they have full-time jobs to get to in the morning.

It will also be your job to make sure the premises remain safe and well-maintained, with gates that lock securely and fencing and enclosures that are free of gaps and sharp edges. When you do detect a breach in safety and security – and you will – you will either have to fix it yourself or hire someone else to do the job. You will also need to have someone come in when you are away to feed and water your horse each day and to make sure all is well.

While at-home horse care may seem a daunting task, it is also one of the most fulfilling and comforting imaginable. How rewarding to know that you are tending to all of your horse's needs personally, and how valuable this can be to the bond you build with your horse! The comfort arises from the familiarity you develop with one another and the control you gain over your horse's all-around well-being. You need not rely on someone else's eyes and efforts to let you know if your horse is ailing or behaving strangely, because you are there. Convenience aside, many a horse owner would have it no other way.

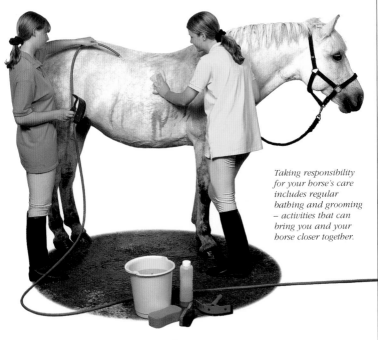

Taking responsibility for your horse's care includes regular bathing and grooming – activities that can bring you and your horse closer together.

TAKE IT SLOW

Whenever you invite a new animal companion into your life, the first few days or weeks are a time of adjustment for both of you. Your goal during the first week of your relationship should not be to break any equine competition records or embark on a week-long endurance trial, but rather to get to know your horse and allow her to get to know you, her new surroundings, and possibly the other horses in her midst.

Think back to your horse's identity as a herd-oriented prey animal and put yourself in her place, suddenly thrust into a strange new environment riddled with unfamiliar scents, people, and horses. Assuming you have chosen your horse wisely and with much forethought and consideration, she will adjust with time, patience, and gentle handling on your part.

Devote your first few days together to helping your horse get acquainted with your touch and your scent. Greet the horse each day with a soft voice, outstretched hands, perhaps a soft blow in the nostrils (a welcome greeting to a friendly, contented equine), and keep activity to a minimum. Spend your time quietly grooming your horse, evaluating what she likes (maybe an apple after grooming sessions) and what she doesn't (having her ears brushed, perhaps).

Go on short walks, guiding the horse by her halter and lead rope, introducing her slowly and gradually to her new environment. Work on establishing your routine and your ground rules right away, because those, too, will offer your horse a sense of security.

FIRST IMPRESSIONS COUNT

If you haven't already done so, you might want to call the veterinarian in to take a look at your horse and evaluate her health and perhaps make sure she is dewormed and vaccinated. It may be wise to wait a while, however, before saddling up and taking a ride. Be patient. There will be plenty of time for that. This is your only opportunity to make a good first impression, and an animal as sensitive as the horse places much stock in those all-important first impressions. Handle the horse roughly, jerk her around in an effort to "show her who's boss," or place too many demands on her from the start, and you'll undermine your own efforts to win your horse's trust – which is the cornerstone of a successful relationship between horse and human.

Be patient and be gentle, and in time your horse will come to welcome you as an important member of her herd. Your presence will begin to be a comfort to the horse, as will the soft nickers of the other horses who share her living space. Just give your horse the time she needs to acknowledge her new herd and new territory. You will be amply rewarded in the end.

GOOD NUTRITION

Take a look at horses in the wild – or even domestic horses that spend their days at pasture – and you discover that the number-one pastime of these great animals is foraging for food and grazing. More than simply a pastime, this is a matter of necessity, because an animal of this size requires a great deal of food, and water, too, to keep her body properly fueled and her system running smoothly.

Before I talk about what and how to feed your horse, it's wise to understand the various nutrients your horse requires for her good health.

PROTEINS

Proteins are the building blocks of such critical body tissues as blood, bone, and muscle – all pretty important tissues to a big, strapping, athletic horse. Providing your horse with high-quality protein, obviously protein derived from plant sources for this quintessential herbivore, is of paramount concern.

FATS AND CARBOHYDRATES

All animals need energy to fuel both internal bodily functions and external action. Fats and carbohydrates supply that fuel (fats are higher in energy than carbs). But supplying a horse with more fuel than she requires can spell trouble in the form of an overweight horse. A companion horse who occasionally takes to the trail and participates in a weekly lesson, for example, will not require as much energy as an endurance competitor or a top-flight athlete who schools and competes every week. Keep fats and carbohydrates in check, and you'll have an all-around healthier, more comfortable horse.

VITAMINS AND MINERALS

Vitamins and minerals are required to maintain bodily functions and ward off disease and illness. They are key players in virtually every important biological process in the horse's body, and must be present in the right quantities and in a proper balance. The two most important factors in the well-fed horse's diet are the quality and balance of the diet, regardless of whether the animal is being fed hay, pasture, hay cubes, grain, or a variety of these feeds.

WATER

We may not think of water as a nutrient, but that is certainly what it is. Horses require a great deal of fresh, clean water each day – up to ten gallons a day, and even more for a hard-driving athlete or working horse. Every horse, regardless of athletic calling, must have constant access to clean, fresh water each and every day. Neglect your horse's watering needs and you invite severe illness and even premature death.

WHAT DO HORSES EAT?

Now that we know what nutrients your horse needs, let's look at the various feeds that supply horses with those nutritional elements. I'll give you a brief overview of the feeds available for horses, as well as some of the special extras you can offer to keep your horse healthy and content.

HAY
The foundation of most domestic horses' diets, hay plays a vital role in nourishing a horse, satisfying her need to chew, and providing the roughage the horse requires to keep her insides running smoothly. Alfalfa hay and timothy hay are the most common hays fed to American horses, but they will work their magic only if they are fresh, sweet-smelling, free of mold and such non-hay components as soil and branches, and consist primarily of leaves rather than stems.

CUBES AND PELLETS
Although they are convenient, hay cubes and alfalfa pellets are processed feeds that are not as high in nutrients as loose hay. They are not as interesting to most horses, either, and don't provide much excitement in the chewing department. Yet they can be a safer alternative for horses with respiratory problems because they are not as dusty as loose hay can be.

PASTURE
A horse's ultimate dining experience is a pasture of rich, nutritious grass, which the animal can explore and graze all day. Of course, not all pastures contain grass of the quality required to properly nourish a horse, and not all horses have the luxury of dining in this manner. But what a treat it is when a horse has the opportunity to do so, even if only occasionally.

GRAINS
Contrary to popular belief, grain is not an appropriate feed for every horse. Oats, corn, and barley are best reserved for horses with high-energy careers that require the extra

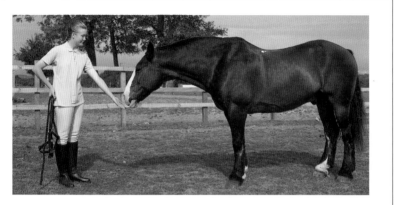

carbohydrates, and thus the extra energy, that grains supply. Horses with special needs, such as those that need to put on some weight or horses pastured outdoors during the winter, may also need some grain.

SUPPLEMENTS

Vitamin supplements are usually best offered only in special circumstances, perhaps when a horse must receive poor-quality hay or pasture, and then ideally under the direction of a veterinarian. But most horses can benefit from a mineral salt block to ensure they receive their full and balanced complement of the minerals they require.

TREATS

Like most animals, horses appreciate having owners who are generous with the treats. Just be careful you're not too generous, or you could end up with an overweight or spoiled equine on your hands. The healthiest treats include carrots and apples, preferably cut into small pieces to prevent the horse from choking. An occasional cup or two of grain also counts as a treat, and of course the ever-popular bran mash. This latter delicacy, best offered once every week or two to the moderately exercised horse, consists of four or five cups of bran, a bit of grain, and some chopped apples and/or carrots, all moistened with some warm water. This is a special treat for a cold winter day.

FEEDING YOUR HORSE

Not all horses are created equal in terms of size and nutritional needs, so not all horses should be fed an identical ration each day. Feed your horse according to her needs and you will keep your companion healthy and fit.

To determine just what your horse requires each day, consult with her veterinarian, who can give you an idea of your horse's weight and whether that weight is appropriate for her frame. Together you can evaluate your horse's work requirements and decide what kind of feed and how much she requires to maintain her health and performance.

HOW TO FEED HAY

Most mature horses of average size – about 1,100 pounds or so – with an average work schedule can usually thrive on two flakes, or approximately eight pounds, of good hay each day. Hay is best and most effectively fed in at least two helpings each day, morning and evening. Three feedings are even better: breakfast, lunch, and dinner.

A haynet should be hung so it is level with a horse's eyes when she is standing naturally. If it's too high, dust and seeds will fall in her eyes as she eats. If it's too low, she may trap her foot in the net.

A water trough must be kept clean by frequent draining and refilling. Don't expect your horse to drink water that you wouldn't drink.

Make sure the hay is offered off the ground, in either a hay rack, feeder or hay net to prevent the horse from inadvertently picking up soil and other bits at mealtimes.

HOW TO FEED GRAIN

Grain rations will depend on what you and your horse's veterinarian determine is appropriate. Grain should be offered in a clean bucket – like hay, never expect your horse to eat it off the ground.

OFFERING WATER

Cleanliness is the name of the game with water, as well. It must be constantly available from a clean, algae-free receptacle, either an automatic waterer or a traditional water trough. Even greater care must be taken in cold weather, when the water can freeze up early in the day. Even a horse outdoors needs her daily ration of water, so you may need to install a safe water-receptacle heater to keep the water flowing.

CLEANLINESS IS THE KEY

How sad it is to see an unkempt horse! Her keepers have forsaken one of the primary tenets of horse ownership: Good housekeeping, and good horsekeeping, must be followed at all times, every day, 365 days a year. See a horse with a dull coat, a tangled mane and tail, neglected hooves, and a face encrusted with discharge from the eyes and nose, and you'll no doubt find this animal in an equally filthy environment. This horse stands amid a thin layer of old straw bedding; an algae-riddled water trough filled with a couple of inches of contaminated water; moldy hay from the most recent feeding strewn about a muddy ground mixed with days worth of manure; and dilapidated fencing that could be taken down with the next big wind. And the horse residing in this mess? Let's just say her misery will be most apparent. Needless to say, you will be doing a much better job with your horse!

Even wild horses know that cleanliness is the key to health and longevity, and they will engage in mutual grooming sessions to help ensure they remain presentable. The domestic horse is at the mercy of her caretakers, though, whose moral responsibility it is to tend to the horse's personal grooming needs and to the environment in which she lives.

Wild horses spend a great deal of time grooming one another. Without a herd of grooming partners, you must wash and brush your horse, from the tip of her nose to the end of her tail.

IT'S UP TO YOU

As you may have guessed by now, this is a huge responsibility, one that you must consider seriously before you bring a horse into your life. There are few animals more demanding in the housekeeping department than the horse, primarily because these are companions who cannot share our own homes. You must not only arrange your horse's living situation, but also make sure every day that it is as clean and pristine as it can be, even if you board your horse at a facility where such chores are supposedly handled by the staff. The ultimate responsibility is yours, and no one will care for your horse as completely as you will.

The same, of course, applies to the horse's personal grooming. This is not simply an issue of wanting everyone to be impressed by your efforts and to remark about your horse's beauty. As the wild horse instinctively understands, it's an issue of survival. A horse is susceptible to a great many parasites, diseases, and injuries, the culprits lurking in the dark recesses of a filthy, unkempt environment just waiting to take advantage of a passing horse whose shabby condition makes her a ripe candidate for attack.

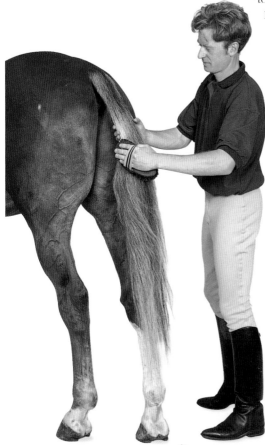

Good house-keeping, then, is another key element in the protection and care of your equine companion – one that requires your daily effort and attention. Neglect it, and your horse will surely suffer.

YOUR EQUINE HOUSECLEANING ROUTINE

Horses thrive best, both physically and emotionally, with owners who commit to regular grooming and a regular environmental cleaning regimen. Your routine, as well as your time commitment, will vary depending on how and where your horse is kept, but either way you will have housekeeping responsibilities. If your horse is boarded, this may involve simply keeping your horse's feeder clean, removing manure from the stall each day and fluffing her bedding. This may seem small, but every little task contributes to the whole picture of a healthy horse in a safe, pristine environment.

The checklist on the next page will offer you guidelines on the tasks involved in keeping a horse's home as clean as it can be.

DAILY CHORES

○ Remove manure and urine-soaked bedding from the stall with a manure fork. Place refuse in a wheelbarrow and dispose of it a safe distance from your horse's home, and as dictated by barn and public policy.

○ Add fresh new bedding, straw, or shavings as needed and fluff with a pitchfork to make a deep, comfortable bed with nice thick edges.

○ Pick up remnants of old uneaten feed – hay, pellets, cubes, and so on – from the ground to prevent spoilage and unhealthy snacking by your horse.

○ Wash feeding buckets.

○ Inspect the water receptacle and clean and fill as needed.

○ Sweep an area around your horse's stall or enclosure to keep dust, which can cause respiratory problems, to a minimum.

ONCE OR TWICE A WEEK

○ Remove all bedding from your horse's stall (whether it's an indoor box stall or an open shelter), wash the floor or rubber mat below with disinfectant, and cover with a thick, deep layer of fresh new straw or shavings.

○ Install fly strips or traps in the stall area to help rid the premises of irritating, disease-carrying flies. Check the strips and traps every few days to make sure they are doing their job.

○ Inspect the premises for safety hazards, such as exposed hardware, fire dangers, broken fencing, sharp edges, or anything in disrepair that could injure the horse or permit escape.

○ Remove manure and poisonous plants from the pasture with the same method used for cleaning the stall.

TACK CARE

The horse's environment isn't all that requires routine cleaning. You will need to pay close attention to your equine companion's tack, as well, to protect both your horse's comfort and your investment in what can be quite expensive equipment. Tack also requires regular inspection and routine care and cleaning. A horse forced to wear dirty tack or tack that is in disrepair is prone to injury, skin problems, and infections. Her rider's and handler's safety may also be at risk.

Keep control over the condition of your horse's tack by first making sure your horse has her own tack; sharing can lead to discomfort and skin problems. Tack should be stored in a clean, dry, secure tack room or shed, where it won't be subject to inclement weather and theft.

Clean the bit with water or mild soap and water, then rinse and dry well after each use. If possible, clean the bridle and reins each time you use them, as well. If you use synthetic tack, you can probably clean it rather easily with a damp sponge or whatever the manufacturer recommends.

THE REGULAR INSPECTION
Make it a habit to inspect the tack thoroughly before or after each use. Periodically inspect all tack surfaces that come into direct contact with your horse's skin: the halter, the bridle, the underside of the saddle and saddle pad, the girth, and so on. Run your hand over the contact surfaces and look for frays, exposed hardware, or anything that might cause your horse discomfort.

Leather tack usually requires a bit more effort. The typical cleaning regimen for leather, which should be done at least once a week, involves first wiping the leather with a cloth, then applying a moderate amount of saddle soap or leather cleaner as directed by the product manufacturer. You may then finish up the job by applying a leather dressing to keep the leather supple.

Metal stirrups and other metal components should be washed and dried thoroughly, and saddle pads should be shaken and brushed to keep them clean, fluffed, and comfortable.

HORSES LOVE TO RUN

As members of a species that has evolved to embody endurance, speed, and strength, horses simply must receive regular exercise. Physical activity is as critical to their well-being as food, water, and companionship.

Exercise provides horses with both physical and mental stimulation. It satisfies that natural equine need for movement and action, born from thousands of years of running in wild bands in search of food over wide expanses of land that hosted predators as well as sustenance.

This tendency was harnessed by people, who demanded hard work of horses as they toiled side by side with humans on the battlefield and the agricultural field, and it continues in the competition world, where horses race against one another in tests

VARIETY AND CAUTION: THE PERFECT PAIR
Variety keeps things interesting for the horse – and for you. To ensure everything remains enjoyable, however, it's wise to have your horse checked by her veterinarian to make sure that participating in whatever you decide is appropriate exercise will indeed be pleasurable and not painful for your equine partner. Once you have this stamp of approval, proceed gradually, allowing your horse to ease into any new activity that may be demanding on her bones and muscles or that could present new experiences, scents, sights, and sounds that require some getting used to emotionally for the horse.

of speed or jumping prowess. Each of these callings has demanded an animal of great physical power and intellectual bearing – two traits that must continue to be addressed and satisfied in our companion horses.

Your horse needs ample time, preferably every day, spent out and about working her muscles and soaking up the sights, sounds, and experiences that make a horse's domestic life fulfilling. Provide your horse with a variety of activities: trail riding on some days, lessons with an instructor in a particular discipline on other days, practice on some days, lungeing and time in the turn-out ring on others, and perhaps occasionally just a quiet walk with you. If it involves the mind and the body, then it qualifies as activity worthy of your horse.

SAFETY FIRST

As much as you may love and admire horses and revel in the prospect of living with them, the fact remains that these animals can pose a very real danger both to themselves and to the people who choose to care for and spend time with them. You can reduce this danger dramatically by practicing basic safety protocols that can help keep you both out of harm's way.

FIRE PREVENTION

You must look out for your horse's safety both at home and on the trail. Good housekeeping habits and vigilant maintenance of the horse's home base (fencing, hygiene, hardware, and tack) can keep the horse healthy and protected from accidents. You should also observe an absolutely no smoking policy anywhere near your horse or her environment, and this should apply to everyone. Make sure, too, that hay and bedding supplies are kept far enough away from the horses so as not to pose a fire hazard, and that fire alarms, smoke detectors, and fire extinguishers are installed in all horse housing areas. Fire is a major safety issue for this species, and horses perish every year in barn fires that could have been prevented.

SAFETY ON THE TRAIL

Protect your horse on the trail by taking her only into familiar areas for which you are convinced your horse is emotionally prepared. Your equine friend may need some practice before carrying you down a city street with noisy traffic or a park that's loud with the squeals and screams of children. Always remain one step ahead of your horse. Be ever alert to potentially scary obstacles

you may find on the trail, such as a fallen tree branch that resembles a snake or an oddly shaped rock that resembles a space alien. Help your horse gradually master such skills as crossing a small creek or walking on rocks, and you'll both end up safer for your efforts.

DRESS FOR SAFETY

Your safety counts, too, and the absolutely greatest step you can take toward protecting yourself is to wear a helmet each and every time you ride, no matter how gentle and reliable your horse is. The horse world is riddled with heartbreaking stories of people who chose not to wear helmets because they were uncomfortable or unfashionable, and who subsequently met a premature end or suffered permanently crippling injuries. Why take chances?

You can further preserve your safety by wearing proper clothing and footwear around horses. This includes boots or special riding shoes that protect your feet and improve your riding. Make sure your horse's tack fits properly to prevent mishaps, too, such as a rider slipping or a horse bucking out of discomfort.

ASSESS YOUR SKILLS

And finally, just as you work on your horse's skills on the trail or in the ring, pay attention to your skills as a rider and equine caretaker. The more skilled and confident you are both in the saddle and on the ground, the less chance you have of sustaining an accident around these potentially dangerous animals.

THE IMPORTANCE OF TRAINING

Training the rider and handler of the horse, as well as the horse, makes life with horses safer and more pleasant. A well-trained horse-and-human team that has mastered the skills of successful interaction between two disparate species has a far more fulfilling and satisfying partnership. Mutual education is the key to greater understanding, more effective communication, and more fun.

You can benefit from learning the nuances of equine care and the ins and outs of a specific riding discipline from a trusted mentor or instructor. You'll then need to hone your skills through practice, practice, and more practice. It can take awhile, for example, to learn the fine art of tying the lead rope properly to restrain your horse securely for a grooming session, or placing the bit smoothly and effortlessly into your horse's mouth, or picking out your horse's hoof thoroughly without fear of a kick. As you master these skills, your horse will learn to cooperate with your efforts – assuming, of course, that you treat your equine partner gently and with respect.

You are wise to pursue a gentle, positive path with your horse as you strengthen your partnership together, and you are wise to find a riding instructor who will treat you with the same respect. With these basic and very positive elements in place, you can watch your bond with your horse blossom. Take the time to learn how to handle and behave around your horse properly, to learn the proper protocols that build not only your own confidence and sense of security, but your horse's as well. There is no better way to convince your horse that you are serious about seeing life through her eyes and are therefore worthy to be trusted. You may just be rewarded with the companionship of an animal who is willing to make similar sacrifices for you.

Trotting on a lunge is a good way to learn the basics of riding under the guidance of an instructor. The horse moves in a circle around the instructor, who controls her from the center with a long rein.

THE HORSE SPORTS

The horse world has many disciplines to appeal to all tastes and all levels of skills, in which you may compete formally or simply work on personally. These include the Western disciplines, such as Western pleasure, gymkhana, and reining; the English disciplines, such as jumping, hunters, combined training, and dressage; and everything in between, from competitive trail riding to endurance riding to vaulting to in-hand halter classes to driving.

Although each discipline is distinct, there are two common threads that run through all of them:
1. Any discipline – and, frankly, any riding – should be pursued only under the guidance of a qualified riding instructor.
2. The ultimate goal should be to have fun.

Master your riding sports skills safely and with consideration for your horse.

Horseback riding is one of the most dangerous sports around. To reduce the risk, take the time to learn how to ride correctly. Anger has no place in your partnership with your horse, especially when it is directed toward your horse. Riding is an ancient art form that can instill a thrill like no other. Keep the experience in the proper perspective, take your time and learn the right way, and you will be a success whether or not you ever win a blue ribbon.

WHAT TO LOOK FOR IN A RIDING INSTRUCTOR

Your instructor can set the stage both for the quality of the skills you develop and your attitude toward your riding and skill level. Choose your instructor according to the guidelines below, and make the most of your own and your horse's potential. Look for:

○ A proven track record both as an instructor and a participant/competitor in your chosen discipline (check references and observe lessons)
○ A positive, supportive attitude toward students and horses
○ A positive and incremental approach to training that emphasizes rewards and praise over punishment
○ An emphasis on safety, including an insistence that riders always wear helmets
○ A humane and loving attitude toward horses (steer clear of those who would beat, berate, or mishandle a horse)
○ Instructor certifications are a definite plus but not a must; though common in the United Kingdom, certifications are not the norm in the United States
○ A willingness to help a beginner learn the basics, from grooming, saddling, and basic handling to horse-show how-tos and protocols
○ Someone with whom you feel comfortable and share a rapport

HAVE SOME FUN

While many people find a great deal of satisfaction in competing formally in various disciplines with their horses, horse lovers do not require organized activities to have fun with their horses. If you're like most equine enthusiasts, just being with a horse is sheer joy. There are plenty of informal activities you can participate in together that don't require your horse to be a high-powered equine athlete in top condition or you to be a world-class rider.

You can spend time together trail riding; in a ring practicing your riding and communication skills; walking together along a trail, up and down the aisles of your boarding stable or even in a local park; doing whatever you feel like doing to satisfy your desire to spend time with your special equine friend.

An unexpected benefit of these informal activities is that they may bring you into contact with other people who share your desire to just spend time with horses. Before you know it, you may find you have made a new circle of friends with whom you can take to the trail or spend time grooming horses and chatting. Simply enjoying your horse's company can prove to be a very social activity, one that can enrich your life in ways you never dreamed when you first decided to live with horses.

LESSONS ARE ALWAYS A GOOD IDEA

Although these informal activities may sound extremely basic, some preparation is in order, as it is for anything your pursue with your horse. Safe trail riding, for example, requires a horse to be trail safe – desensitized to the unexpected surprises she may encounter when she's out beyond the security of her home environment, such as dogs, other horses, or chattering kids on bicycles. And if you enjoy spending time in the ring practicing silent leg signals, or leg aids, with your horse, you'll need to know how to perform these correctly. You are thus wise to take lessons from a qualified instructor to become a skilled rider, no matter what your plan to do.

THE LANGUAGE OF HORSES

The greatest gift you can offer your horse – and the best way to strengthen the relationship you share – is to make an effort to learn the equine language. Your horse is a member of a very complex and intelligent species, with a distinct language that is part of the successful social relationships that for eons have been the foundation of their survival. Take the time to learn that language by observing the horses around you – yours and others – and spending time with your horse.

Horses communicate through a combination of body postures and vocalizations. I'll tell you about a few that you are likely to observe in the course of your interactions with your horse.

VOCALIZATIONS

Visit a busy boarding stable and you will hear a variety of equine calls as you wander up and down the aisles. The traditional neigh, for example, is typically used as a call from one horse to another, usually when one member of the herd has been separated from another. Feel complimented if you are greeted with a nicker from a horse, as this soft, gentle sound is reserved for those few individuals with whom the horse shares a special bond. On the other hand, a snort is the horse's response to fear or alarm, so do what you can to reduce the circumstances that inspire such a sound, whether the perceived threat is real or imagined.

Fright or fury is being communicated by these horses.

The horse on the left displays his dominant status to the youngster on the right.

THE EARS

For a barometer of your horse's mindset at any given moment, look at her ears. A horse who is alert and curious will typically hold her ears at attention, high, pricked, and pointed forward. A horse's content-ed, relaxed dem-

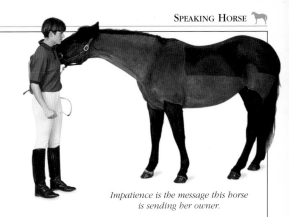

Impatience is the message this horse is sending her owner.

eanor will also be reflected in her ears, which will seem almost flopped over, even pointed backward. Beware the horse who pins her ears back against her head, however, and keep your distance, for a horse with this undeniably aggressive ear position is about to bite or similarly lash out, either at you or at another horse.

THE EYES HAVE IT

The eyes are the windows to the equine soul, so look into your horse's eyes for clues to what she's trying to tell you – especially when her expressions are combined with ear position and other physical signals. If you can clearly see the whites of a horse's eyes and note a high head position and tense muscles in the neck, you've got a frightened horse on your hands. A natural, relaxed expression in the eyes reveals a calm and contented horse, while a horse at attention or a bit more agitated will follow the object of her attention carefully with her gaze to ensure that the object does not become a threat.

BODY LANGUAGE

The horse skillfully uses her body and muscles to communicate a vast equine vocabulary. A tail held high and carried like a flag is the sign of an enthusiastic and exuberant horse, for example, while a horse who paws the ground and throws her head up and down is impatient and perhaps agitated or ill. And the bucking horse? That very graphic body language could mean the horse is feeling healthy and spirited, or is in pain. Or perhaps the horse is simply trying to dislodge the rider on her back. It's your job to translate the meaning of the message within the given context and in combination with other signals. The better you know your horse, the better translator you will be.

HORSES, KIDS, AND OTHER ANIMALS

Horses are social animals who thrive among their own kind, yet they live in a world populated by herds of non-equine creatures. Many of these are predatory animals – dogs and humans come to mind – and the domestic horse is forced to coexist with these predators every day on the trail and even at home. You can help make this daily existence easier on your horse by preparing her to tolerate, and even enjoy, the presence of animals that might otherwise instill natural fear in this classic survival-minded prey animal.

The horse who is best equipped to deal with the everyday surprises that life holds is the horse who has been exposed to a variety of other animals – other horses, dogs, cats, and people of all ages – in a positive way and, preferably, under your close supervision. Introduce your horse to people (including children) you trust who know how to behave around horses, and to dogs who are trained to behave properly around the equine species. Reward your horse with praise, strokes,

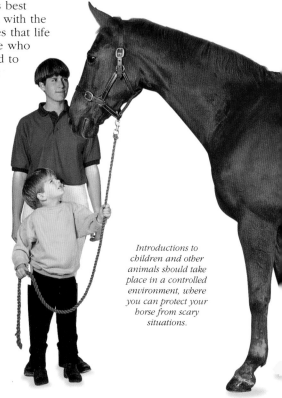

Introductions to children and other animals should take place in a controlled environment, where you can protect your horse from scary situations.

and treats for her tolerance of
these new acquaintances,
and gradually increase the
duration of the meetings. In
time you could have the
friendliest horse in town.

Of course, some horses come to their
owners with a history of negative
experiences. You will have to work
on rehabilitating the animal who has
been the victim of, say, young children
who pull on manes and tails, or dogs that nip
at equine heels or bark aggressively in the presence of horses.
Rehab could take time, so be patient with your horse and respect
her unhappy memories and very real fears.

If you live with children and dogs as
well as horses, it's your
responsibility to train your
children and dogs to behave
properly in the presence of
the equine members of the
family. Their interactions
should be supervised, and
mistreatment must not be
tolerated.

It is also your responsibility,
as your horse's guardian, to
acknowledge your horse's
weaknesses and to watch out
for the animal's well-being.
Don't lead your horse into
situations – a birthday party
with fifteen screaming four-
year-olds, for example – that
she is not emotionally
prepared to handle. Be fair
and protect your horse from
unnecessary stress.

GROOMING EVERY DAY

A well-groomed horse is beautiful, healthier, and more comfortable. The coat, mane, and tail, and even the face of this animal are clean and free of dust, mud, plant materials, and other irritants. Her feet are less likely to cause her pain or discomfort. She can more comfortably wear tack. Her skin, with oils properly distributed, is healthier and less prone to invasion by parasites. Maintaining that well-groomed appearance and reaping its considerable benefits, however, requires the efforts of a very dedicated owner who understands the many responsibilities of grooming and commits to them on a daily basis.

Routine grooming is a must for the healthy, properly cared for horse, and a

The beautiful, healthy look of a horse like this doesn't happen by magic, nor does it happen overnight. Only a major commitment to regular grooming makes a horse look this good.

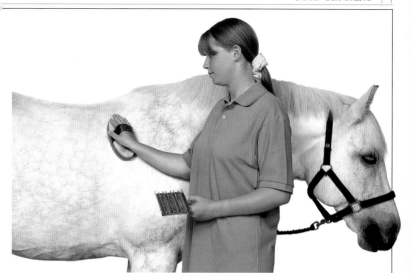

profound bonding experience for you both. The secret is to groom your horse from head to tail to feet each and every time you are together, whether you are riding that day (ideally brushing your horse both before and after the ride) or just visiting your horse at the boarding stable. Only with such constant attention can you create the breathtaking vision that is the right of every horse: the gleaming coat, the flowing mane and tail, the bright facial expression.

AN INVESTMENT IN HEALTH

In addition to creating a vision of beauty, your commitment to grooming is also an important investment in your horse's health. Regular grooming gives you the best education possible in what is normal for your horse and what isn't. When you are familiar with the contours of your horse's muscles and structure from neck to legs to hindquarters, the texture of her coat and skin, and the overall condition of her eyes and ears, you'll notice instantly (probably during a routine grooming session) a strange bump on her neck or a thick discharge from her eyes. As any veterinarian can tell you, the sooner you spot such conditions and seek treatment, the better chance the animal has of recovering with minimal pain and discomfort.

YOUR GROOMING ROUTINE

The following is a suggested routine covering the basics of good grooming. In time you will develop your own order and rhythm, all guided by your commitment to groom your horse thoroughly and frequently.

○ Place a halter with a lead rope on your horse and tie the horse securely to a post or bar where you will be grooming her.

○ Carefully lifting each foot, gently yet thoroughly clean out the underside of each hoof with the hoof pick. Avoid the softer, blood-rich, V-shaped section of the hoof called the frog; poking it could damage the foot and prove painful to the horse.

○ Run the rubber curry comb in circles all over the horse's body to remove shedding hair, dried mud, dirt, and anything else caught in your horse's coat.

○ Brush the horse's body, from head to legs to hindquarters, with the stiff-bristle brush to remove all dirt and foreign bodies. This could be quite a job if your horse has been pastured. Allow any mud on the coat to dry before brushing it out.

○ Clean the hair from the brush after every few strokes by rubbing it against the rubber curry comb.

○ Brush the horse's face and ears gently with the soft-bristle brush.

○ Gently swab the horse's face with a damp sponge or cloth. Pay close attention to the eyes and nostrils to remove crust, dirt, mud, discharges, and so on. Use one sponge or cloth for the eyes and a separate one for the nostrils to prevent spreading infection.

Use a hoof pick that is not too sharp. When picking out the hoof, first clean the grooves beside the frog, then clean the sole of the foot. Always work toward the toe to avoid damaging the frog.

○ With a separate sponge, clean the horse's dock (the area beneath the tail).

○ Brush the mane, forelock, and tail with the mane-and-tail brush.

○ Once a week or so, clean a male horse's sheath and a mare's udder with a damp cloth or sponge set aside solely for that job.

○ Apply fly spray or other repellent as needed and as directed.

If you will be bathing your horse, do so only on a warm day. Tie her securely, and apply shampoo with a cloth or sponge. Rinse the horse thoroughly with a hose or water from a bucket (avoid the ears and face), remove excess water with a sweat scraper, then walk the horse around to dry her coat completely.

As you brush the mane, you can remove any tangles with your fingers.

Carefully brush any dirt and debris out of the tail.

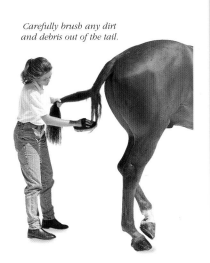

YOUR GROOMING TOOLS

The first step in your grooming routine is to gather the necessary equipment. The basics of your grooming kit will include:

○ Brushes, one with stiff bristles and one with soft

○ A rubber curry comb

○ A hoof pick

○ A mane-and-tail brush and comb

○ Cotton balls

○ Sponges

○ Equine shampoo

○ A sweat scraper

○ Fly spray and/or wipes

○ Soft cloths and towels

HOOF CARE

To paraphrase an old saying, without a healthy hoof you have no horse. While a horse is certainly more than the sum of her hooves, the feet are of paramount importance to the health and overall comfort of the animal. You can promote your horse's foot health by ensuring that in addition to your own routine care of your horse's feet, you also enlist the regular services of a good farrier, or blacksmith.

Without regular care and attention, the hooves can become overgrown (like overgrown fingernails) and packed with mud, manure and dirt, ultimately resulting, most cruelly, in a horse in excruciating pain who can hardly walk. A dedicated owner will work hard to clean the feet regularly, and will call in a farrier to keep the feet properly trimmed, and, if necessary, shod. A skilled farrier can maintain the health of a horse's hooves and even help to relieve the pain and discomfort of a horse with foot problems through special trimming and shoeing techniques. Sure this can get expensive, but it is simply another routine expense you must take into account when you choose to live with a horse.

Frog
Cleft of frog
Seat of corn
Horn
Sole

Heavy draft horses have big, broad feet with long hair down the pasterns that's called feathers.

FINDING A FARRIER

You and your farrier each play important roles in the care of your horse's hooves. In addition to cleaning the feet daily (both before and after riding, if possible), you should also work to make your horse a cooperative candidate for the farrier's attentions by keeping the animal calm and helping her to relax in the face of new and unusual experiences. As for the farrier's role, while not every horse (especially not those with exceptionally hard hooves) must wear shoes, the farrier should be enlisted to trim the feet and to inspect them for potential problems every six weeks or so. Look for a farrier who genuinely enjoys the company of horses, who approaches his or her time-honored tasks as a vocation, who handles horses with respect and affection, and who appreciates just how important his or her job is to the overall health and well-being of your horse.

YOUR EQUINE VETERINARIAN

People who live with horses are lucky. Unlike dogs and cats, who have average life spans of a dozen years or so, a horse can live into her twenties, and possibly even hit the thirty-year mark and beyond. But this will only happen if the horse enjoys years of proper care and the good health that results.

You, of course, play an important role in maintaining your horse's health and vitality, but you're not alone in this mission. Horses are prone to a variety of illnesses, health conditions, and injuries, so through the years you will find that one of your greatest assets is a skilled and trusted equine veterinarian. While your horse's regular care is your responsibility, you will rely on the veterinarian for those various health services, routine and otherwise, that only a professional can provide. The veterinarian, in turn, will rely on you to be the first line of defense in your horse's care. It's your job to know what is normal for your healthy horse, and be prepared to seek professional help as soon as you notice a change in your horse's condition.

Not all veterinarians are created equal, so do your homework when choosing the practitioner to whom you will entrust the health of your precious equine friend. Ask fellow horse owners for recommendations, and observe for yourself how veterinarians at your boarding stable handle their patients. It's usually pretty easy to spot who the good ones are.

WHAT TO LOOK FOR IN AN EQUINE VETERINARIAN

The following criteria should help you in your quest for a good equine veterinarian. Look for:

❍ An experienced individual with an excellent educational background who specializes in the care of horses
❍ Good word-of-mouth recommendations from other horse owners
❍ A vet who makes house calls
❍ Reasonable fees (but be aware that equine veterinary care can be expensive) and payment plans for larger expenses
❍ A responsive and professional staff
❍ A genuine love of horses and a gentle way of handling patients
❍ A willingness to answer your questions and to give you as much information as possible about your horse's condition
❍ An emphasis on preventive medicine
❍ On call nights and weekends; when not on call, find a vet who provides clients with an emergency number
❍ Someone with whom you share a rapport

When you're choosing an equine veterinarian, ask for references and be sure to check them.

PREVENTIVE CARE

The cornerstone of a sound equine health care regimen is your own commitment to a preventive care program. Observe your horse carefully, follow all the tenets of responsible equine care, and call the veterinarian not only when you suspect a problem with your horse's health, but also for routine veterinary visits, just to make sure all is well with your horse. The following guidelines will help you cover the bases in carrying out your horse's preventive care program.

DEWORMING

A horse's world is riddled with internal parasites – worms – which she may inadvertently pick up from the ground while grazing or munching on her afternoon hay, or which may be transmitted by such external parasites as those ever-present flies. While you probably cannot prevent infestation entirely, you can keep worms at bay by instituting a sound deworming program. The frequency of deworming treatments will depend on where you live and the types of worms prevalent there. As with vaccines, it's best to carry out your horse's deworming under the guidance of your veterinarian. She or he will not only help you determine when your horse requires treatment, but also help to ensure that the treatment is safe and effective.

VACCINATIONS

There are vaccinations that most veterinarians recommend for all horses regularly, and those that are typically recommended only for horses in certain areas where the diseases are common. Those on the "must" list are tetanus, equine influenza, rhinopneumonitis, eastern and western encephalomyelitis, and strangles. Depending on where you live, your veterinarian may also recommend vaccines for Potomac horse fever, rabies, anthrax, botulism, and Venezuelan equine encephalomyelitis. These vaccines are best administered by your veterinarian, who can guarantee the vaccines' quality and make sure they are administered correctly.

TEETH

If a horse is going to live to see her thirtieth birthday, she has to have good teeth to keep her nourished through the years. Equine teeth are designed to keep growing and changing throughout a horse's life, but if they do not wear properly in the process, they can cause the horse pain, illness, and malnutrition. A dental examination is thus an important part of the routine veterinary examination. The veterinarian will examine the horse's teeth to determine whether they require floating. A procedure a horse may require as often as twice a year, floating involves filing down sharp edges that could be interfering with the horse's chewing action and comfort.

GENERAL CARE

All the tender loving care you offer your horse in routine grooming, exercise, hoof care, nutrition, environmental housekeeping and, of course,

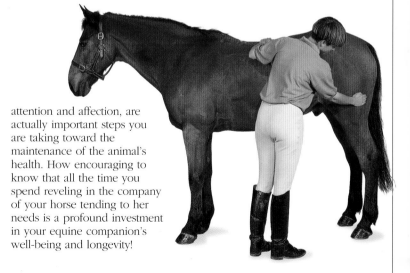

attention and affection, are actually important steps you are taking toward the maintenance of the animal's health. How encouraging to know that all the time you spend reveling in the company of your horse tending to her needs is a profound investment in your equine companion's well-being and longevity!

WHEN TO CALL THE VET

Entire books have been written about the diseases and health problems that can afflict even a healthy, well cared for horse, but you need not memorize the pages of those volumes to ensure your horse receives the proper care she needs in the event of an emergency. Instead, acquaint yourself with the signs that can indicate equine illness or injury, and be prepared to call the veterinarian when the need arises. When you do notice such signs, you can further help your horse by remaining calm and keeping your horse confined to her stall or similarly restrained.

This veterinarian is checking the horse's hooves and shoes for the cause of sudden lameness.

SIGNS OF EQUINE ILLNESS

What follows are the classic signs that a horse is ailing and needs help. Whenever you even suspect a problem, do not hesitate to call the veterinarian. Even if the situation ends up being a false alarm, you have done your horse a great service. Look for:

- ○ Loss of appetite; an outright refusal to eat or drink
- ○ Diarrhea
- ○ Apathetic, depressed demeanor, and the body language to match
- ○ Discharge from the eyes or nostrils, or an eye the horse cannot open
- ○ Difficulty urinating or defecating; straining behavior
- ○ Obvious signs of discomfort and pain, such as pawing at the ground; sweating; fidgety body movements, such as violent tail swishing, biting at the flanks and kicking at the stomach; pacing; and an inability to remain standing or lying down (all of which are the signs of colic and require immediate veterinary attention)
- ○ Obvious signs of injury, such as a bleeding wound, an inability to stand, a favored leg, and swelling anywhere on the body
- ○ Respiratory distress (labored or rapid breathing, or noisy, congested breathing)
- ○ Inability to stand, move or walk properly
- ○ A lack of skin elasticity and dry mucous membranes (signs of dehydration)
- ○ A dull, dry coat, and dry, scaly skin
- ○ Lumps and bumps on the skin
- ○ Limping or lameness
- ○ Coughing or choking

YOUR HORSE NEEDS YOU

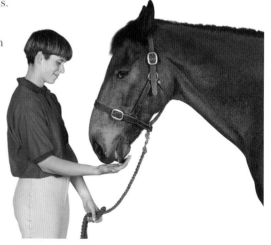

Within the world of companion animals, horses not the easy keepers. These are large animals with potentially tricky temperaments, dangerous habits, voracious appetites, inconvenient housing requirements, and an expensive lifestyle. Yet horses are also the stuff of which dreams are made.

And just what do we owe these animals for the unique magic they bring into our lives? Well, good food, regular grooming, routine health care, exercise, and all that, but aside from the intensive care and expense we must invest into their long-term well-being, we owe them our love and affection. Contrary to popular (and inexperienced) belief, these are the greatest gifts we can offer our rather non-traditional animal companions.

Throughout the centuries, although they have not always been treated humanely while in our care – a fact made abundantly clear in Anna Sewell's book *Black Beauty* – horses have also worked handsomely with

us as partners, as though our bond were somehow preordained, somehow meant to be those many thousands of years ago.

On the surface, and certainly to the untrained onlooker, horses may seem aloof to our attentions and our affections, maintaining their noble, dignified demeanor in the face of our hugs, tickles, embraces and, in some cases, baby talk. But those who live with horses know the truth. We understand the unspoken bond that can blossom between a horse and the people she loves. The bond must be experienced to be believed, but it is awarded only to those who make the great sacrifices required to become honorary members of the equine family. Proving oneself worthy of so high an honor takes time, so be patient, do your work, and you may just be rewarded with a horse's undying loyalty and affection. There's nothing else like it.

MORE TO LEARN

The horse world is so vast and so diverse, it would be impossible to present a complete list of all available horse resources – there are whole libraries devoted to the subject. The following, however, should give you a good start in your quest to learn more about the horse.

ORGANIZATIONS

American Association of Equine Practitioners
4075 Iron Works Parkway
Lexington, KY 40511
(606) 233-0147
www.aaep.org

American Horse Council
1700 K Street, NW #300
Washington, DC 20006
www.horsecouncil.org

American Horse Protection Association
1000 29th Street, NW #T-100
Washington, DC 20007
(202) 965-0500

United States Pony Clubs
4071 Iron Works Parkway
Lexington, KY 40511-8462
(606) 254-7669
www.ponyclub.org

BOOKS

The Complete Horse Care Manual, by Colin Vogel, BVM, Dorling Kindersley Publishing

The Encyclopedia of the Horse, by Elwyn Hartley Edwards, Dorling Kindersley Publishing

Horse Owner's Veterinary Handbook, Second Edition, by James M. Giffin, MD and Tom Gore, DVM, Howell Book House

Horses for Dummies, by Audrey Pavia, IDG Books

The Kingdom of the Horse, Caroline Davis, consulting editor, Howell Book House

Lyons on Horses, by John Lyons, Doubleday

The Man Who Listens to Horses, by Monty Roberts, Random House

MAGAZINES

Equus
656 Quince Orchard Road
Gaithersburg, MD 20878

Horse Illustrated
P.O. Box 6050
Mission Viejo, CA 92690
www.catfancy.com/horses/default.asp

Horse & Rider
1597 Cole Boulevard, #350
Golden, CO 80401

WEB SITES

All About Horses
members.xoom.com/abouthorses/

Alternative Veterinary Medicine
www.altvetmed.com

American Veterinary Medical Association
www.avma.org/care4pets

Equines of the World
www.geocities.com/Heartland/

Ranch/8841/

The HayNet
www.haynet.net/

HorseNet
www.horsenet.com

The Shagya Arab originated in Hungary from Arabian stock.

ABOUT THE AUTHOR

Betsy Sikora Siino is an award-winning author, who has written almost twenty books and hundreds of articles on animals – all kinds of animals – and their care. Some of her most recent books include *For the Life of Your Dog* (with Olympic gold medalist Greg Louganis), *The Complete Idiot's Guide to Choosing a Pet*, and horse breed books on the Thoroughbred, the Arabian, and the American Quarter Horse. In addition to her concern for the care and well-being of the world's companion animals, Betsy has a special interest in children and animals, the human-animal bond, and the preservation and survival of wild species.

INDEX

Dorling DK Kindersley

LONDON, NEW YORK, SYDNEY, DELHI, PARIS,
MUNICH, JOHANNESBURG

Project Editor: Beth Adelman
Design: Carol Wells, Annemarie Redmond
Cover Design: Gus Yoo
Photo Research: Mark Dennis, Romaine Werblow
Index: Nanette Cardon

Photo Credits: Geoff Brightling, Gordon Clayton, Andy Crawford, Kit Houghton, Bob Langrish, Ray Moller, Stephen Oliver, Tim Ridley, Jerry Young

Thanks to the following horses and their owners: pg.2: Swedish National Stud; pg.6: Royal Veterinary College; pg.12: Bengad Dark Mullein, Mrs. C. Bowyer, Symondsbury Stud; pg.32: Wellington Riding Ltd.; pg.33 Teton, Wild Horse Research; pg.34: Golden Nugget, Sally Chaplin; pg.46: Shaker's Supreme, Fred & Bonnie Neuville, Kentucky; pg.50: Sjolike, Sonia Gray, Tattonda Carriages; pg.61: Kemir, Bablova State Stud, Hungary; pg.64: Nemo, Ileen Poole, Canada

First American Edition, 2000
2 4 6 8 10 9 7 5 3 1

Published in the United States by
Dorling Kindersley Publishing, Inc. 95 Madison Avenue New York, New York 10016

Copyright © 2000 Dorling Kindersley Publishing, Inc.

All rights reserved under International and Pan-American Copyright Conventions. No part of this publication may be reproduced, stored in a retrieval system, or transmitted in any form or by any means, electronic, mechanical, photocopying, recording, or otherwise, without the prior written permission of the copyright owner. Published in Great Britain by Dorling Kindersley Limited.

Dorling Kindersley Publishing, Inc. offers special discounts for bulk purchases for sales promotion or premiums. Specific, large-quantity needs can be met with special editions, including personalized covers, excerpts of existing guides, and corporate imprints. For more information, contact Special Markets Department, Dorling Kindersley Publishing, Inc., 95 Madison Avenue, New York, NY 10016 Fax: (800) 600-9098.

Color reproduction by Colourscan, Singapore
Printed in Hong Kong by Wing King Tong

Library of Congress Cataloging-in-Publication Data
Siino, Betsy Sikora.
What your horse needs / Betsy Sikora Siino. — 1st American ed.
p. cm. — (What your pet needs)
Includes index.
ISBN 0-7894-6525-6 (alk. paper)
1. Horses. I. Title. II. Series.
SF285.3 .S55 2000
636.1—dc21
00-008284

See our complete catalog at
www.dk.com